Bill Clinton

By ELAINE LANDAU

FRANKLIN WATTS

NEW YORK ★ CHICAGO ★ LONDON ★ TORONTO ★ SYDNEY

For
perhaps the first woman president . . .

Cover photograph copyright © Mike Stewart

Photographs copyright ©: Wide World Photos: pp. 2, 54; Stocktrek Photo Agency: p. 8; The Clinton Family: pp 11,12,15,19,24; Sygma/Mike Stewart: pp. 16, 42, 49; Unicorn Stock Photos/ Richard C. Reed: p. 17; David Sams: pp. 21, 37, 38, 53; Leo de Wys Inc./Fridmar Damm: p. 27; Mike Stewart: pp. 28, 36, 44, 51; Light Sources, Stock/Paul Rocheleau: p. 30; Photoreporters, Inc./Evan Richman: p. 32; Sygma: pp. 34, 46; Reuters/Bettmann: p. 47; Stacy Rosenstock: pp. 50, 52.

Library of Congress Cataloging-in-Publication Data

Landau, Elaine.
   Bill Clinton / by Elaine Landau.
      p.   cm.
   Includes bibliographical references and index.
   Summary: Details the life of Bill Clinton, from his formative years to his tenure as governor of Arkansas, and focuses on his 1992 presidential campaign.
   ISBN 0-531-11143-1 (lib. bdg.). — ISBN 0-531-15670-2 (pbk.)
   1. Clinton, Bill, 1946–   —Juvenile literature.   2. Presidential candidates—United States—Biography—Juvenile literature.
                  3. Governors—Arkansas—Biography—Juvenile literature.
   4. Presidents—United States—Election—1992—Juvenile literature.
   [1. Clinton, Bill, 1946–   2. Presidents.]   I. Title.
   E840.8.C57L36   1993
   973.92—dc20
   [B[92-35763   CIP   AC

CONTENTS

BORN IN ARKANSAS

November 3, 1992, was a proud day for Arkansas. The state's forty-six-year-old governor, Bill Clinton, had just been elected president of the United States. As our first president from Arkansas, he would be the forty-second man to hold the nation's highest office.

Becoming president was a goal that Clinton had long dreamed about and worked for. Some people who knew him as a young man felt that he would go far. However, the Arkansas governor was not born with a silver spoon in his mouth.

Clinton's parents, William Jefferson Blythe III and Virginia Cassidy Blythe, were a young couple of modest means who had married in the early 1940s. At age twenty-seven, Clinton's handsome father had been an automobile salesman from Sherman, Texas, who had recently moved to Shreveport, Louisiana. There he met Bill's mother, a student nurse at the city's Tri-State Hospital. Clinton's mother later described their meeting as love at first sight.

Yet shortly after their wedding, the young couple was forced to separate. With the outbreak of World War II, Blythe entered the service. When he returned three years later, he faced the prospect of few jobs, along with thousands of other former servicemen.

After an exhausting search, Blythe finally landed a position selling construction equipment in Chicago, Illinois. His new job required him to travel throughout much of middle America. But even when he was far from home, Blythe frequently drove two to three hundred miles a night to be with his wife.

As Blythe's sales territory expanded, it became increasingly difficult for him to return home as often. Since Virginia was expecting a child, she temporarily moved in with her parents in Hope, Arkansas. Meanwhile, her husband looked for a house for them in Chicago.

Within several months, Blythe found the ideal place for his growing family. He excitedly set out to bring his wife to their dream home, but he never reached Arkansas. On the way, his car crashed into a ditch, and he was thrown from the vehicle. William Blythe died that night off Highway 61 in Sikeston, Missouri.

On August 19, 1946, three months after her husband's death, his widow gave birth to a son. She named the boy William Jefferson after his father; people often remarked on how much the boy looked like him.

Virginia Blythe knew it would be difficult for her to raise the boy on a nurse's salary, so she left her young son with his grandparents while she trained at Charity Hospital in New Orleans to become a nurse-anesthetist. This advanced training would enable her to earn more money. Separating from her child proved to be extremely difficult for Mrs. Blythe. Bill Clinton later described his mother's departure at the train station this way: "I remember my mother crying and actually falling down on her knees by the railbed. And my grandmother saying, 'She's doing this for you.' "[1]

Clinton's grandparents owned a small grocery store in the African-American section of Hope, Arkansas. Although Clinton only spent the first few years of his life with them, his grandparents greatly influenced the boy's values and ideals. Both were firm believers in the importance of learning and education. In addition to giving the child a strong religious background, they taught him to read and count. By the time he was three years old, Bill Clinton could read short books on his own. It was already clear to those around him that he was a special child.

As a boy, Clinton was taught to be polite. His grandmother firmly believed that a well-mannered, respectful child was bound to be successful.

GROWING UP

By the time Clinton turned four, his mother had both completed her advanced nursing courses and remarried. The boy's new stepfather was a car dealer named Roger Clinton. Mr. Clinton soon moved the family to the resort town of Hot Springs, Arkansas. As expected, his stepson did extremely well in school there. However, his parents were surprised when he once brought home a report card with all A's except for a D in conduct. When his mother went to school to see what the problem was, Clinton's teacher replied:

"Why, there's no real problem; it's just that . . . he is so sharp and he's so alert . . . he knows the answer immediately, and he will not give the others a chance. . . . I have to get his attention one way or another. And this is the only way I know to do it because he is so competitive he will not be able to stand his D.''[1] His teacher was right and the eager young boy soon changed his behavior.

For much of his early life, Clinton's mother
divided her time working as a nurse and caring
for her family. Here, years later, she spends a
moment relaxing with her dog.

Facing page: *Hot Springs, Arkansas, where Clinton
lived with his family, was a southern resort town.
Its natural springs were a popular tourist draw.*

When Bill Clinton's family moved to Hot Springs, he attended a small Catholic school even though his family were devout Southern Baptists. At age nine, he was switched to public school.

Although Clinton excelled in school, his home life wasn't without difficulties. When he was ten, his mother gave birth to his half brother, Roger. Clinton enjoyed being with and looking after the child. As a teenager, he even legally changed his last name from Blythe to Clinton, so his brother would not begin school with a different last name.

The family's happiness was somewhat marred by Roger Clinton, Sr.'s, serious drinking problem. Unfortunately, after having too much to drink, Clinton's stepfather sometimes became violent. Once he even fired a gun in the house. As Bill Clinton grew older, he felt he had to protect his mother and Roger, Jr.

During one of his stepfather's outbursts, Clinton stepped between the drunken man and his mother and half brother and

said, "You will never hit either of them again. If you want them, you'll have to go through me."[2] Roger Clinton, Sr.'s, violence stopped, but his drinking did not. And even though he and Clinton's mother often separated, after a time, they always reunited.

In spite of his often stressful home environment, Clinton still did well in many areas of his life. He took up the saxophone and became an outstanding young musician. Tackling every type of music from the classics to jazz, Clinton won first place in a statewide high school competition. His music teacher recalled the talented student tenderly playing the saxophone as though it were a violin.

Although Clinton enjoyed a wide range of activities, his true love was politics. Even as a nine-year-old, he eagerly watched the political conventions on television as well as followed Washington happenings in the papers. In 1963, at the age of seventeen, Clinton attended Boys' State—a summer program where high school students study politics and government. There he was elected as a delegate to Boys' Nation. This meant he would go to Washington, D.C., with delegates from around the country to see the American political process in action.

In addition to visiting various historic sites and politicians' offices, the students were taken to the White House. Clinton even had a chance to meet and shake hands with his idol— President John F. Kennedy. Bill Clinton never forgot that experience. Before his Washington, D.C., trip, he considered becoming a Baptist minister or a musician. But when he returned home, he told his mother that he was determined to go into politics.

*In July 1963, seventeen-year-old Bill Clinton
served as a Boys' Nation delegate and met
President John F. Kennedy.*

Some who knew Clinton might have already guessed as much. The young man's competitive nature and leadership qualities were clearly evident early on in his life. When he was only eight, the family's housekeeper thought Clinton should become a minister so that he could lead others to God. Later on, he became active in school politics, serving as president of his junior class. As a high school student, Bill Clinton was also involved in various civic groups.

His friends and neighbors felt that Clinton's sensitivity toward people might make him the type of politician America needed. As a young boy his mother had once sent him to the store on Thanksgiving Day to pick up a few last-minute items for their meal. On his way out of the store, Clinton stopped to talk to a small boy sitting alone on the store's stoop. After learning that the child had nowhere to go on Thanksgiving, Clinton brought him home to share the family's dinner.

Bill Clinton's interest in people continued as he grew older. Clinton dated local girls and had a fair number of friends. After school and on weekends, they often spent time playing their instruments together or going to the movies. Clinton also enjoyed backyard football and basketball games, yet one of his friends later recalled that Clinton was not quite as athletic as he would like to be remembered. This may have been partly because he was somewhat overweight as a young teen.

Clinton never allowed his outside activities to affect his grades. He was a member of the National Honor Society and a National Merit Scholarship semifinalist, and he placed fourth in a graduating class of 323 students. Looking back on those

*Bill Clinton graduated from Hot Springs
High School in 1964. He was a favorite
of a number of his teachers.*

years, Clinton noted that the memory of a father he had never met had been a driving force in his life. His natural father's untimely death had made Bill Clinton keenly aware of how quickly life can be snatched away. He was determined to accomplish all he could, since he often felt as though he were living for both himself and his father.

By the time he was ready to enter college, there was little doubt that Bill Clinton was headed for an important role in America's future. As one of his high school teachers put it: "I just haven't seen anything quite like it in my teaching experience. There have been other bright people for sure, but Bill Clinton just has it easily head and shoulders above anybody in leadership ability."[3]

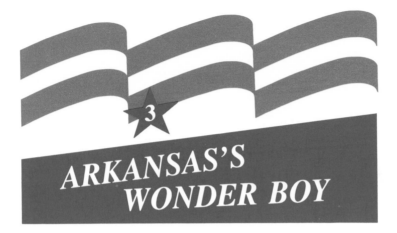

ARKANSAS'S WONDER BOY

In the fall of 1964, an eighteen-year-old Bill Clinton excitedly prepared to leave for his freshman year of college. He was entering Georgetown University in Washington, D.C.—the only school he had applied to. Clinton chose Georgetown for several reasons. The university had a fine reputation and Clinton's high school guidance counselor thought it an excellent place to study politics. The teenager had also dreamed of attending college in the capital since visiting Washington as a Boys' Nation delegate. Clinton wanted to eventually return to Arkansas to participate in state government. He hoped his Washington, D.C., experiences would enhance his ability to serve.

Bill Clinton found his Georgetown classes extremely exciting. He had rarely left Arkansas in the past, but on campus he met professors and students from around the globe. As in

Clinton enjoyed attending college in
Washington, D.C. In addition to learning
a great deal, he made many new friends.

high school, his leadership qualities soon emerged. While majoring in international affairs, Clinton was elected class president in both his freshman and sophomore years.

The forty-second president's college days were hardly carefree. Tuition at Georgetown University was high, and the Clinton family could hardly afford the costs involved. During the school year and summer, Clinton took part-time jobs to help meet expenses.

He was often quite skilled at getting the best wages for himself. That was obvious when he applied for a job in Arkansas senator William Fulbright's Washington, D.C., office. After convincing Fulbright's assistant to hire him, Clinton was offered the choice of two types of jobs. He could either have a full-time job at $5,000 a year or a part-time job for $3,000. But Bill Clinton asked for a third option. He said, "I'll take two part-time jobs."[1] He got what he asked for.

The clever college student still had to face some painful situations. In 1967, his stepfather, Roger Clinton, Sr., was admitted to Duke University Hospital in Durham, North Carolina, for cancer. The doctors told the family that he didn't have long to live. In spite of their past problems, Bill Clinton loved his stepfather and wanted him to know that. For the last six weeks of Roger Clinton's life, Bill Clinton frequently traveled two hundred fifty miles to be with him. The experience was rewarding for both of them. Clinton later described his feelings:

"I think he knew that I was coming down there because I loved him. There was nothing else to fight over, nothing else to run from. It was a wonderful time in my life and I think in his."[2]

After graduating from Georgetown, Clinton won the prestigious Rhodes Scholarship. The money allowed him to study at Oxford University in England from 1968 to 1970. It was the first time Clinton could afford to concentrate on his studies without having a part-time job.

During these years, Bill Clinton was forced to deal with a personal conflict that later resurfaced in his 1992 bid for the presidency. While Clinton was in England, organized opposition to the Vietnam War raged in the United States. Like many young men of his generation, Bill Clinton loved his country, but he felt that U.S. involvement in the war was wrong.

During his first year at Oxford, he received a letter from his draft board asking him to report for duty. But since the date he was to appear had already passed, Clinton wrote to the board asking how to proceed. At that point, Clinton was granted a draft deferment until the end of the school year.

When Clinton returned to Arkansas that summer, he considered not going back to England for his second year at Oxford. Instead, he thought he might attend the University of Arkansas's law school while enrolling in the Reserve Officers' Training School (ROTC) there. This would allow him to train for the military while earning a law degree.

But Clinton's critics later charged that his ROTC enrollment was merely a ploy to avoid the draft. They argued that since Clinton was preparing for eventual military service in the ROTC, he would probably receive a student deferment until he completed law school. His opponents stressed that by then the war was likely to be over.

Yet as it turned out, Bill Clinton chose another path. He canceled his ROTC agreement and returned to Oxford after

*At twenty-two, Bill Clinton attended Oxford
University in England. His surroundings were quite
different from what he had been used to in Arkansas.*

Although Clinton did not serve in the Vietnam War, years later as Arkansas's governor, he became commander-in-chief of the Arkansas National Guard.

all. While this once again made him eligible for the draft, he was never called to duty. That's because the government had begun selecting its army recruits through a draft lottery. When he left for Oxford, Clinton had no way of knowing if his number would be chosen—it wasn't.

Clinton's last year at Oxford was exceptionally enriching. He traveled extensively, took a variety of courses, and read over three hundred books. But still another incident occurred at that time that later also proved to be a political handicap. During his last year in England, Bill Clinton smoked marijuana once or twice. Claiming not to have liked it or even to have inhaled, he later publicly stated that his drug experimentation stopped there. Nevertheless, during his 1992 presidential campaign, opponents used this episode to discredit him.

After leaving Oxford, Clinton headed for New Haven, Connecticut. He had been offered a scholarship to Yale Law School and was anxious to begin his studies. Although he had always been an exceptional student, going to law school would not be easy for Clinton. In addition to taking classes, he needed three part-time jobs just to meet the expenses not covered by his scholarship.

Yale was one of the best law schools in the country. But it was also important to Bill Clinton for another reason. That was where he met Hillary Rodham—the woman he later married. Hillary Rodham's background differed from that of her future husband's in many ways. Raised in the affluent Chicago suburb of Park Ridge, she was the only daughter of a well-off fabric store owner. While Bill Clinton had long been against social injustice and favored the Democratic party, Hillary Rodham came from a conservative Republican family.

*After returning from England in 1971, Clinton went
to Yale Law School (shown here). He met his wife,
Hillary, at the library there.*

Yet even before she had finished high school, Rodham had begun to change her views. As a teenager, she was greatly influenced by her Methodist minister, who encouraged frequent exchanges between suburban young people and inner-city youths. He also set up a church program through which teens baby-sat for migrant workers' children. She remembers the minister telling her youth group that "to be a Christian did not just mean you were concerned about your own personal salvation."[3]

When she left for Wellesley College in the fall of 1965, she was still a Republican. But as a student Hillary Rodham soon became interested in such social issues as poverty, education, and the government's responsiveness to the people. These concerns had long been championed by both the Democratic party and Bill Clinton—whom she would meet several years later.

Hillary Rodham did extremely well in college. She was well liked, earned high grades, and served as student government president. Her success continued after she entered Yale Law School. She was editor of the highly thought of *Yale Law Review* as well as another journal. Rodham was even given her own key to the library for late-night research and study.

She and Clinton met and dated in law school, but did not marry immediately. Instead, after graduation, the two lived in different parts of the country for a time. Clinton returned to Arkansas to pursue a career in state government. Rodham worked as a staff attorney for the Children's Defense Fund in Cambridge, Massachusetts.

She then moved to Washington, D.C., where she served on the House Judiciary Committee. It was the summer of 1974

In 1992, years after her own graduation,
Hillary Clinton returned to Wellesley College
to address students there.

and the committee was looking into possible wrongdoing by former President Richard M. Nixon. Rodham worked diligently on the committee. Although she had become a Democrat, those serving with her noted that "she kept politics out of it."[4]

During this time, Rodham remained in touch with the special young man she had met in law school. There were numerous calls and visits, and in 1974 Bill Clinton asked her to marry him. He had said, "I know this is really a hard choice for you because I'm committed to living in Arkansas."[5]

It *was* a difficult decision for Rodham, who had spent much of her life in northern urban centers. Bill Clinton was the first person she had ever met from Arkansas. Although her friends liked him, they joked that she would be going off to the ends of the earth. But Hillary Rodham decided to "follow her heart" and move to Arkansas to marry Bill Clinton. In no time at all, she fell in love with the state and its people.

Bill Clinton's political career there was already well under way. At twenty-seven, he ran for Congress against a Republican incumbent thought to be unbeatable. Clinton did not defeat him, but he came closer to doing so than any Democrat ever had. From then on, Bill Clinton became known as the "wonder boy" of Arkansas politics.

The title fit Clinton well. Unlike politicians who disliked campaigning, Clinton thrived on it. He enjoyed speaking to voters and explaining his views on important issues. Once in a while on the campaign trail he stopped his car at a roadside construction site. Moments later, he had gathered together the workers to ask for their votes.

*As a newly married couple, Bill and Hillary Clinton
set out to build a life together in Arkansas.*

People throughout the state enjoyed his warmth and openness. They also soon became confident of his ability to lead. By 1976, Bill Clinton had won his first state victory. He was elected attorney general of Arkansas.

Clinton worked tirelessly as the state's lawyer. He fought against unfair price increases by large businesses. Clinton was also credited with stopping the utilities from raising their rates. He eased prison overcrowding by broadening the state's work-release program. Under this system, inmates left the prison to hold day jobs. They only returned to the detention center at night. The program also better prepared inmates for their release.

Although Clinton was successful as attorney general, he hoped to go further. Now considered a political rising star, he ran for governor in 1978. It was a difficult race, but Clinton's campaign team was extremely well organized. He won the election, and at thirty-two became America's youngest governor.

Bill Clinton enthusiastically entered office eager to enact reforms. However, he soon learned that turning ideas into action wasn't always easy in government. Clinton had been especially anxious to improve Arkansas's school system. He had hoped to combine small school districts into larger ones throughout the state. But his plan was poorly received by most of the smaller districts, and many state legislators representing those areas actively fought against it. Realizing that it would never pass, the young governor eventually withdrew the bill.

Clinton's "car tag" tax also proved extremely unpopular. This legislation raised fees on car registrations and title transfers as well as gasoline and tire tax rates. The money was to

*Here, one of Clinton's youngest fans
holds a campaign sign.*

As a young, energetic candidate, Bill Clinton
seemed like a politician who would go far.

After losing the 1980 election for governor,
Clinton told voters to "remember me as one who
reached for all he could for Arkansas."

be used for a much-needed highway repair program. However, the taxes angered many of the state's poorer residents who felt its impact hardest.

At times it seemed as if the new governor couldn't do anything right. Some people were even outraged because his wife had kept her maiden name instead of changing it to Clinton. Critics claimed that Clinton and his young idealistic staff had tried to do too much too soon. They stressed that Clinton's assistants had been too hard on utilities and the business concerns that often keep politicians in power. Clinton's attempts to improve life in Arkansas were further hampered by the poor economic conditions affecting the rest of the country. Whatever the reasons, Bill Clinton lost his 1980 bid for reelection to his Republican opponent.

Hillary Rodham had been working at a law firm in Little Rock since 1977. Now the former governor began practicing law himself. Friends noted that following his defeat, he had become somewhat depressed. At a very young age, Bill Clinton had achieved more than many people do in a lifetime. But now the "wonder boy" of Arkansas politics had taken a hard fall.

MAKING A COMEBACK

Despite his 1980 election loss, there was still a shining moment in Bill Clinton's life that year. On February 27, 1980, his only child, Chelsea Victoria, was born. The new father was thrilled with his little girl. He felt blessed to be able to experience what his father had never had an opportunity to do—hold his child in his arms.

Before long, things began to look up politically for the former governor as well. People seemed interested in his views, as Clinton began to once again address civic groups and other organizations around the state. Then the former governor took a daring step. He ran a television ad stressing that he had learned from his past mistakes and wanted to run again in 1982. The ad received a great deal of public attention.

People began to see Bill Clinton as a more mature and seasoned candidate. Now, when speaking in public, he patiently listened to his audience's thoughts and feelings.

Some felt that if reelected, Bill Clinton was likely to give voters what they wanted rather than what he thought they needed.

Clinton won the 1982 election with 55 percent of the vote, becoming the first Arkansas governor ever to be defeated and then later returned to office.

By the close of his new term, Governor Clinton had accomplished much to be proud of. He set out to dramatically improve public education in Arkansas and he succeeded. Now he eagerly looked forward to another term in office to accomplish even more.

The governor's success, however, had been somewhat dampened by a family problem. Unfortunately, his twenty-eight-year-old half brother, Roger Clinton, Jr., had become involved in an illegal drug operation. The state police brought the matter to the governor's attention after realizing who one of their prime suspects was. Putting his personal feelings aside, Clinton told the police to continue their investigation.

Following his arrest, Roger Clinton, Jr., pleaded guilty to the charges against him. He served just over a year in a federal prison. The turn of events deeply upset Bill Clinton. Although he tried to appear self-confident, he was often depressed. There was talk of marital problems between the governor and his wife, and even gossip that Clinton had been seeing other women.

After his half brother's prison release, the entire family went into counseling. This helped Bill Clinton to come to terms with some painful feelings he had pushed aside for years. Having an alcoholic stepfather had been extremely difficult, and Clinton often said that he had to act as if he were forty when he was just sixteen.

*Bill Clinton poses for a picture with his
half brother, Roger. Although Roger's arrest
was difficult for the family, the young man
managed to turn his life around.*

During this emotionally rocky period, the governor still had to prepare his reelection campaign. Yet despite his personal difficulties, he won another term in office. In 1984, for the third time in his life, Bill Clinton stood on the steps of Arkansas's capitol building taking the governor's oath of office.

As before, Clinton pressed for education reforms. His wife continued to be quite helpful to him in this area. She headed an education panel that successfully toured the state, raising support for her husband's plans. While Arkansas had formerly ranked poorly on state spending for education, Clinton worked diligently to change matters. The governor established competency tests for teachers to make sure that they were qualified. Parents were also fined for failing to attend important parent/teacher conferences.

As governor, Clinton also worked actively to increase business opportunities within the state. He offered attractive tax breaks to encourage businesses to relocate in Arkansas. Through the state's Industrial Development Commission, loans were made more readily available to new businesses. Clinton also pursued measures for welfare (public assistance) reform and worked for firearms restrictions.

Two years later, Bill Clinton ran for his fourth term as governor. He easily won the 1986 election with 64 percent of the votes. The Arkansas legislature had recently lengthened the governor's term from two to four years, so now Bill Clinton was expected to serve until 1990.

Some people doubted that he would do so. As early as April 1987, the Arkansas governor told reporters that he might try to win the 1988 Democratic presidential nomination. But

The Arkansas governor and his wife, Hillary,
enjoy a dance at a glamorous evening gala.

by July of that year, he had decided against it. His daughter was only seven years old at the time, and he and his wife did not want to leave her to campaign nationally. Long ago, Clinton had made an important promise to himself. He vowed that if he were fortunate enough to have a child, he would never be an absentee father. He put off his political future to keep his word.

In 1990, Bill Clinton ran for a fifth term as governor of Arkansas. He won, becoming the state's first governor to serve five terms in a row. Clinton publicly stated that he wanted to remain in office because there was still much more to do.

Clinton remained an important national figure. He served as chairman of the Democratic Leadership Council—a group of moderate Democrats hoping to bring the party back to the political center. Clinton was often described as a new breed of Democrat—someone who might be able to unite the liberal and conservative elements of the party.

On October 3, 1991, Bill Clinton announced his candidacy for president. He faced a difficult primary campaign against a number of impressive rivals. Clinton visited various states, speaking about his plans for the country while debating opponents. After winning the majority of state primary elections, he received his party's nomination at the Democratic National Convention in July 1992. Bill Clinton would challenge Republican incumbent President George Bush in the November 1992 election, and independent candidate, H. Ross Perot.

Clinton knew it would be a difficult contest to win. Charges of his having smoked marijuana and having dodged the draft were raised by opponents. The situation was worsened when it was revealed that, unknown to Clinton, his

*Clinton always cared about children and
education. While governor of Arkansas,
he achieved the largest budget increases for
public education in that state's history.*

*Presidential candidate Clinton, his daughter,
Chelsea, and his wife, Hillary, react with their
supporters after watching the state of Ohio put
Clinton over the top to win the Democratic
party nomination at the convention in
New York City in July 1992.*

uncle had tried to persuade the draft board to defer his nephew. Once again rumors of the Arkansas governor being involved with other women surfaced. To help clear the air, Bill Clinton appeared on national television with his wife. The couple stated that although they had had some past marital difficulties, they were committed to making their marriage work. Clinton later told reporters, "We never wanted to give up on each other, and we still don't."[1]

Bill Clinton forged ahead with his presidential campaign. Political observers frequently commented on his remarkable ability to take hard punches and keep coming back. The candidate chose the popular Tennessee senator Albert Gore, Jr. as his vice-presidential running mate. Gore was well respected for his environmental work. The two men campaigned throughout the country, making their views known. Clinton came out in favor of military budget cuts, improved health coverage for workers, tax cuts for most Americans, and reduced energy use.

Clinton was pro-choice, stating that the decision to have an abortion should rest with the woman and her doctor. He also favored expanding the college-loan program. Clinton suggested that in the future these loans might be repaid through national service or long-range personal payment plans. If elected president, he also hoped to place medical clinics in the public schools. This way young people would be certain to receive health care.

In 1992's poor economy, Bill Clinton was an appealing alternative. He told voters: "I believe with all my heart that the future of our country is on the line. That is why these [his suggestions for change] are not just economic proposals. They

*Here, Chelsea Clinton, accompanied by her cat,
attends an outdoor event.*

*On the campaign trail, Bill Clinton speaks
with young people outside Thomas Jefferson
High School in New York City.*

The Clinton and Gore families greet voters
during the 1992 presidential campaign.

At a public library in the Harlem section
of New York City, Bill Clinton asks adult
literacy students for their votes.

are the way to save the very soul of our nation.''[2] Many of
those who had long felt ignored by President Bush's adminis-
tration and policies—women, minority group members,
young people, and workers—were swayed by Clinton's dream
for the nation's future.

The Arkansas governor won the 1992 presidential election
with a decisive victory. Polls showed that he did extremely

*Clinton chats with a senior citizen on one
of his many 1992 campaign stops.*

well in areas formerly thought of as Republican strongholds.
No matter how difficult the path to the White House became,
he never turned back or gave up. Early in his political career,
Clinton developed his own formula for success. As he had
simply put it: "You have to be able to take a lot of criticism—
suffer defeats, and get up tomorrow and fight again."[3] It
proved to be a winning method for the forty-second president
of the United States.

★*53*

President-elect Bill Clinton reaches into a crowd of supporters as Hillary Clinton and Tipper Gore (right) cheer at the Old State House in Little Rock, Arkansas, on election night.

SOURCE NOTES

Chapter 1
1. Donald Baer, ''Man-Child in Politics Land,'' *U.S. News & World Report* (October 14, 1991): 40.

Chapter 2
1. Charles F. Allen and Jonathan Portis, *The Life and Career of Bill Clinton: The Comeback Kid* (New York: Birch Lane Press, 1992), 6.
2. Bill Turque, ''I Think We're Ready,'' *Newsweek* (February 3, 1992): 21.
3. Ibid., 8.

Chapter 3
1. Donald Baer and Steven V. Roberts, ''The Making of Bill

Clinton," *U.S. News & World Report* (March 30, 1992):
29.
2. Charles F. Allen and Jonathan Portis, *The Life and Career
of Bill Clinton: The Comeback Kid* (New York: Birch Lane
Press, 1992), 24.
3. Bill Turque, "I Think We're Ready," *Newsweek* (February
3, 1992): 21.
4. Kenneth T. Walker, "The Hillary Factor," *U.S. News &
World Report* (April 27, 1992): 34.
5. Turque, op cit.

Chapter 4
1. Eleanor Clift, "Political Ambitions, Personal Choices,"
Newsweek (March 9, 1992): 36.
2. Jim Moore, *Clinton: Young Man in a Hurry* (Fort Worth,
Texas: The Summit Group, 1992), 236.
3. Charles F. Allen and Jonathan Portis, *The Life and Career
of Bill Clinton: The Comeback Kid* (New York: Birch Lane
Press, 1992), 18.

GLOSSARY

Absentee. A person who is absent or away.

Anesthetist. An individual trained to administer anesthetics, drugs that deaden pain.

Attorney general. The chief law officer of a country or state. In the United States, each state has an attorney general.

Boys' State. A citizenship-training program sponsored by the American Legion. Students learn how government works by running a make-believe government.

Conservative. A political philosophy emphasizing order, tradition, and minimal government action in the private sector.

Draft deferment. A status preventing an individual from being drafted, called to serve in the armed forces. With the present volunteer army in the United States, the draft no longer exists.

Incumbent. A person holding an office.

Infidelity. Breaking marriage vows.

Liberal. A political philosophy promoting freedom and equality. Liberals approve of government action to achieve social and economic well-being.

National Honor Society. An organization for students from tenth to twelfth grade. Members are selected on the basis of their grades, leadership, service, and character qualities.

Primary election. An election held by a political party to select a candidate to represent it in the general election.

Rhodes Scholarship. A highly regarded award sponsoring outstanding scholars to study at Oxford University in England.

Title transfer (car). Transferring the official ownership of a motor vehicle.

FOR FURTHER READING

Adler, David A. *A Picture Book of John F. Kennedy*. New York: Holiday House, 1991.

Climo, Shirley. *City! Washington, D.C.* New York: Macmillan, 1991.

Faber, Doris. *Eleanor Roosevelt: First Lady of the World*. New York: Viking, 1985.

Fradin, Dennis Brindell. *Washington, D.C.* Chicago: Childrens Press, 1992.

Heindrich, Ann. *Arkansas: America the Beautiful*. Chicago: Childrens Press, 1989.

Hewett, Joan. *Getting Elected: The Diary of a Campaign*. New York: Lodestar, 1989.

Kent, Zachary. *George Bush: Forty-First President of the United States*. Chicago: Childrens Press, 1989.

———. *Ronald Reagan: Fortieth President of the United States*. Chicago: Childrens Press, 1989.

Sandak, Cass R. *The Franklin Roosevelts*. New York: Crestwood House, 1992.

Wade, Linda R. *James Carter: Thirty-Ninth President of the United States*. Chicago: Childrens Press, 1989.

INDEX

ABOUT THE AUTHOR

Elaine Landau received a BA degree from New York University and a master's degree in library and information science from Pratt Institute. She has written over fifty books for young readers, including the biographies *Robert Fulton* and *Colin Powell: Four-Star General*.

Ms. Landau makes her home in Sparta, New Jersey.